Poems from Macoma Beaches

Poems from Macoma Beaches

Stanley Sackeyfio

Gulf Coast Publications
Texas

Dedicated to Karen Scott and my parents
Joseph T. Sackeyfio and Effua Taylor

Poems from Macoma Beaches
Gulf Coast Publications
Dallas, Texas

Gulf Coast Publications
ISBN 978-0-9883257-2-2
® TXu 1-962-474

Printed in the United States of America

Poems from Macoma Beaches

Collected Poems 1996-2014
Table of Contents

Poems from Macoma Beaches

Introduction

Born in Ghana, Stanley Sackeyfio was exposed to poetry in his formative years at Mfantsipim High School by Christopher Barlow, Gordon Green and Joe De Graft Johnson. After graduating with a degree from the University of Central Oklahoma, he received a post-graduate degree as well in Business Administration.

Through the years, he maintained his avid interest in poetry, and enjoyed works of British and American poets, particularly works by Dryden, Keats, Baron, Angelou, Dickerson and Browning, to name a few.

The collection of short poems is a tribute to the poets, play writers, short story writers and novelist that preceded him. It is also his contribution to the continuation of storytelling using poetry as genre, and encouragement of the next generation of readers to do the same.

Poems from Macoma Beaches

A Soldier's Search for Identity

Who you are, and who I am
Depends on how I
Know and accept myself.

Walking towards the desert dune
I came upon a date-ringed oasis
Where I paused to ponder
The winding railed rivers
That slide life to its sodden end.

And as I sat in the shaded silence,
Dew of the date-drenched tree
Began to patter my top;
A brash desert bee buzzed
Notes of the howling wind
Porting dust to a dune pyre.

A Sahara ant stung a gnat
Right before my eyes
And, in an instant, lost all
It was or could have been.

A rare desert rain fell in torrents
To awake the burrowed lungfish
From its long, long sleep
To complete a life cycle
And recoil in the mud-filled hole
Without a trace as the rain raced on.

A gaggle of agile grunts
Mounded sand castles to honor
The listless who chose safety of home
Over the safety doldrums of war;

A soldier's helmet and a bayonet
Meant to protect or maim.
Lay apart like severed limbs;

A chance encounter with a foe
Fighting for ill-defined cause
And the outstretched hand
Begging Grace for a paid killer;

The napalm salvoes fired to bury
The brave and the wounded left
To honor graveyard pit.

The cracked whip meant to crush
A people's search for freedom,
Incites rats to squabble over scraps
Ere the wise embrace blood
The selfless spilled for country.

A shepherd floated a ditty
To amuse privileged men
Who breed, and sleep, and
Tether their children to havens
While chancing others to answer
The drumbeats of war when evil
Is lauded and the sage are singed.

I saw masked men manning posts;
Handheld chiefs in regaled caftans
Beginning to debate how
Vanity instructs us to choose glib
And wind bagged flattery,
Or open pride and opulence
Strain the well of human kindness
When triumph defines our vanity
And faith steers us beyond
The aegis of surrender and guidance.

I heard wounded hearts plead
To the posted sentry at the edge
Of life; the free and unbridled,
Sharing the calming warmth
Encircling human failings;
The lustful fresh exposing isolation;
The delightful beauty trickling
Through to join charity with
Self-discovery and self-acceptance.

Poems from Macoma Beaches

Attainment

Wither we go or stay
Wither we peruse
What is true and real
Attainments remain
Seamless pauses in phantoms for an opera.

Youth treads the tumid path
Like the floating flamingo
But you, my traveling friend
Must follow the raying sun
Like conscience trails the eastern star
Till you reach the shore and all is done.

You set your goals at the mooring
When swallows swapped posts
With hanging bats, and the dawn
Began to mimic dusk; and
The sun mirrors the falling moon
To birth a brand new day.

Perhaps you solved a riddle
Formulated by happenstance
And thoughtfully designed intuit
To invite us to a pyre atop a kiln
Set for the damned souls,

And like many before whose pride
Was etched by a stone adze,
You raised your broken wings
To scribble a note or two
For wayside fiddlers to play.

You pranced with your kinfolks
To build hovels for the newborn;
Only to watch them destroyed
Before you crossed the Rubicon
To a recluse trapped in miasma
To know the value your gift.

You heard the tom-tom's muzzled notes;
The quaver and the noggin-brick
Pitted against the righteous will.
The villain poised against virtue;
The fidelity of the final note meant
For an unconscionable deist
Who cast his lot with an atheist.

The victor of a victimless crime
Came to your door and claimed discovery
Of desiderata; and like a venerable soul
You looked at the exhibit and nearly saw
Novelties birthed to serve decadence;
The human beast in venerable forms;
The sagacious imp and the imbecile
Struggling for an unreachable end.

Yet, through it all or in spite of it,
The avid grave digger labors on,
A heap of sodden shovel at a time;
A clod of sod and trowel dirt;
A pile of gravel and heap dirt;
Progress in measurable mites;
Compressed chain of endless thoughts
Which time transmutes in micro bits
From one generation to the next.

The novel and transiently aged
Trading the past for the present
Placing the tested with the untested
To reach endless starts
Fit for the scraggy scalawags
Of an unmarked tombstone
Hidden from the fledged idealist.

Cricket Melodies

Uneasy lie the voices that sing differing tunes
To a fluid crowd that is too busy to enjoy
The eternal melodies of your scrambled scales.

The earth sank under the load of the ardent heat
To summon the barn owl to an early feat,
As the furry rabbit busily gathers nuts to reel
And crickets chirr defiant tunes from the keel.

A housemaid cleaning the pots for hearty meal
Debates which spices will give the food a real
Taste and which ones are passé for a parrot
Wrestling with chirring crickets over a carrot.

Noise replaces silence as the day transforms
Itself to serve men and women in mini forms
Aristocrats in serape savor wine and eat caviar
As the cricket begins to chirr blessings to avatar.

The rain falls on all dead and living creatures
Teachers look for answers tied to old lectures.
But the beautiful butterfly flaps in the cove
To free the gray-colored cricket from a glove,

The moon melts into ambers of the rising sun
The town flounders when firemen begin to run
So the fire spreads to kill those that give a heck
About a scandalous cricket chirring for a check.

The winding surfs recede with sea waves
To reveal buried homes in the sandy coves.
But, farmhands walling pupae from escape
Can still hear crickets cheering from the cape.

Everywhere we turn at dawn, noon or dusk
Busy, happy or sad people work without mask
They do what needs done in misery minuets
To delightful crickets chirring in mini-duets.

The igloo walls in cold and frozen climes
Is far, far away from the tropic hot domes
But, the six-legged cricket finds a way
To awaken the worm with its creaky sway

The cricket chirrs in the tropic heat after the rain
The cricket chirrs in the winter cool after the drain
And everywhere you go North, South, East or West
The chirring cricket can quickly jars much needed rest.

Chirping crickets have a knack for passing each hour
With discordant, irreverent, irritating arias that dour
Our senses or summon us on the strike of five
To rescue our beloved Queen Anna from the hive.

Eudaimones

Contentment is illusive to
The restless who know neither peace nor harmony.

Tethered to the drives of daily living,
People of blessed homes cannot hear
The echoes from plaintive drums;
War and the threats of war rain on every land;
The living do not heed the grieving dead,
And everywhere the quivering strings of Poesy
Are lost on cultures poised at the precipice
Of hate, discourse, and force over fellow man.

Sapless clutter zaps the soul's search for solitude.
Idleness lures you to lie in the eddies of forlorn glory
That is soon lost to the abyss like irretrievable arkites.
Moneyed nations look at the poor ones and say:
"Their hardship is harped on natural selection."

A rustic hand pedals Beauty to a people
Set on exacting formulae and reviewing details.
Euclidian theorists ponder why Socrates debated
The pros and cons of an ideal society
With unsophisticated sophists bent on
Holding views contrary to true justice.

Uncertain times test our fervent resolve
To control uncontrollable portends
Only to find a world pitted on pillaged peace
Beseeching time for sonorous solitude;
Or exposed the mediocre, the less endowed,
That clap cymbals to attract attention and
Make the simple tasks appear more odious.

Happiness flies on the wings of joy
To accept pretense as real, and
Heap hollow honors on widened wallets

Condemning compassion and integrity
To advance the welfare of its charge,
And transit innocence of the unborn
To a society searching for a true purpose.

Miscreants are assigned choice seats.
Minions watch receding moments beg
Salutations from a convoy of Pundits
Lay claim to a hermit with knowledge
And reputation assigned to the few
As Voltaire reviews measures for welts
At the behest of rhesus monkeys known for
Rehearsing plays set in hollow willows.

A culture deeply seeped in its success
Is soon trapped in the wilderness
Like the lonely nomad who gave up
His craft before its time because
A seasoned judge known for fairness
Grossly miscarried justice
And stripped conscience of
Its fair minded nature
To rule for the unjustly damned.

Religion duped Ptolemy into believing
His discovery was devoid of scientific facts.
The simple and impenitent romantics,
Seek refuge with thoughtful philanthropists;
The hungry holds vigil at the homes of the rich
Yet, through conflicting passion and dispassion,
The ax joins the social with the solitary;
The unending search for relevance and meaning,
Death ushers birth to life's ring.

The desire for oneness and separateness;
Aloneness and belonging drives cultures
And people everywhere toward Eudaimones,
Where the wind, freed by the nymphs,

Whips the waves into the open arms of utopia,
The unsung hero of true love and easeful harmony,
Rekindling our faith in what we could be.
Oh! What Keshena!

* Eudaimones was the blessed human state of ancient Greece.

Poems from Macoma Beaches

Faces

Let's enjoy faces like these or those
Faces that amuse or frighten us;
Faces that sag with sadness;
Faces that mask their true nature.

What faces do I see?
Do I see the faces of suited sailors dancing with wolves
Or maidens floating fancy free atop winding waves;
The humming, quivering, rumbling, rippling waters
Meandering, winding, settling on a peaceful note?

And the draught came
Fraught with blame.

What faces do I share?
Do I share faces filled with sorrow and hope
Roaming half-deserted streets for a fair hearing;
The solemn faces assuming the mantle of justice;
The quiet and simple stance exuding faith and trust?

The face of justice
The face of injustice.

What faces do I hold?
Do I hold withered faces of the aged or newborn;
Lovely faces filled with compassionate care
The wretched bony face writhed like a prune
The puffed ego of a sultry soul bowing to fleeting fame;
The resurrection of the past set afloat on fading mist?

And they were ready to grope
For the Cape of Good Hope.

What faces do I glean?
Do I glean faces of honed or untold horror
Spreading hatred among nations and peoples they meet,
Pitiable orphans eking scraps from social bins;
Cragged mothers poised to accept shame as fit reward;
Usurious lenders exacting payments from helpless debtors?

The end began anew
For the blessed few.

What faces do I hide?
Do I hide the faces of shame in sinful poses?
Goodness wrapped in pain at unexpected places
The mortal Medusa marbled as Bodhisattva ,
The communicant priest, sells dogma to a sane society?

The sane living among the insane
The terms designed for the inane.

What faces do I spy?
Do I spy friendly faces opening doors at dawn
To welcome one and all to a daily feast;
Propose toast in memory of the past and what lies ahead,
And watch aloneness spitefully consume Goodwill?

The good will go over the hump
Evil will lose grip on the bump.

Yet on the pale and spotless faces
Visions vie with revision for space
The child within yearns for love and comfort
The adult within craves acceptance
The lame and the sick seek cure and compassion
Repentant souls do their best to right wrongs
The dependent struggles for strength
The palm reader cajoles tales from jokers.

Beauty will join with the ecstatic
To prevail over joy and the majestic.

.

From Here to There

Seek fun
In its manifestations
Even as you express your uniqueness and
Oneness with nature and fellow man.

From here and there
Funny things happen everywhere and
People make funny things happen.
Passages of time turn moments into
Fear and hope or pain or joy.
We laugh and cry to ink
Our common bond and
Weave cloth of varied strands
Into a unified human race
Of shared values and beliefs;
Merging our past with the present
Separating darkness from light, and
Darkness from silhouette.

A man in Bengal appears
Indifferent to an event in Nepal
Because it's irrelevant to his life
Likewise, the misfortune that befalls
The iguana of the savannahs
May seem as different as sari
To a nomadic tribesman roaming
The dusty dunes and rocky hills
Of the Sahara or an emote to a Fijian, who
Fathoms his good fortune insulates
Him from the woes of the indigent,
Whose penury pegs them
Like a quarryman grinding quartz
To eke life from lifeless stones.

Farmers blame their losses on the soil
But the calumny clouds hold
To a different point of view;
Bad or good, new and not so new
Gray or clear, ashen and dark

Rainbow colors and unshaped
Moving at a leisurely pace
Oblivious to the pain or pleasure
Yet ready to birth life through rain.

Rainfall and flowered plants
Like John's head on a platter
Helped a King keep his word,
But, an alchemist seeking cure
For the common cold cried out
For Hippocrates to excise hate
From the hurt and wounded
And return outcasts to the main.

Priesthood built on empty vows
Like mighty mansions on sand
Lose ordination to the old and witty
And ask youth and the savvy vole
Why lust allures fiendish-flesh
Into its selfish ways.

Yet, from here to there
Or there to here,
In many places and many ways
All creatures big and small
Birthed in high and low places
Spread fun everywhere
For everyone who cares to pause,
To taste joys brought for one and all.

The sparrow with its painted plumage
Skips across the colorless sky
As snowflakes laden with water
Turns into gentle rain and
Fall softly on the hardened sod
To birth the dawn of a new year.

Sweet zithers and even vespers
Open leaves and plant boughs
To buzzing-bees and busy bodies
As the sun warms the earth

For fruitful-life and new surprises
Or hold the world in warm embrace.

Moving melodies and moving waters
Ripple over pebbled ponds
To end torture for bleeding souls;
As the rising moon and the falling sun
Rouse volcanoes to spew lava
For destruction and renewal
Wherever they tread.

For, from here to there
Or from there to here
Zestful life and beauty
Await discovery and enjoyment
By every man and beast
Ready to drink nature's delights.

If Only

The endowed gift is often ignored.

If only I could see the world
Through the eyes of a child;
Think of it with the mind of an adult,
And accept it with the wisdom of Simeon,
I would be whole.

If only I could give all I have to just causes;
Live in interminable joyful moments;
Accept who I truly am, and
Meld peace with the conflicts of my soul,
I would be whole.

If only I could love in unfettered grace;
Admire the perfection of creation,
The imperfections I see in me, and
Smile when unexpected chances unfold,
I would be whole.

If only I could through my will
Change what I am, and will my desires
To stem simmering doubts, and
Celebrate each man's life in my own,
I would be whole.

If only I could live in peace with myself
And wish peace for different others
Or live in harmony with the phases of man,
And accept each man's creed as real
I would reduce human conflicts
And be whole.

If only I could part my needs from wants
View everyman's struggle in my own
And forgiveness as true gifts
I would see beauty in its varied forms
Peg envy to its unenviable place
And live in joyfulness of the whole.

If only I could be steadfast when tested
Hear the unheard and unspoken at each hour
Confess every man is integral to the tapestry
I would celebrate each moment as the last,
Stand with the afflicted and the cast off,
And be counted as part of the whole.

Passages

The beginning
Presses along the winding path
To a plinth where a graying parrot lives.

Joined by the seamless flow of time
The mist of happy, joyful beginnings
Mirrors the sad and joyless endings
Toddling steps guide the growing child
The graduated eddies steady the teen
To spirits readied to rebirth life anew

The mid passage is often fraught
With roil, and broil, and soil
The urge to join or be let alone
The inveterate drive to drill or foil
The eternal search for a post

Leases were taken or left to wither
Friendships made or fallowed;
Bridges built or broken
For new ventures and fresh faces
That end with the dome saying

"The bell tolled and called for you
The bell tolled and called for me
The falcon did not hear the falconer
The hunted the hunter
For the restless wind muzzled
The stealthy steps of the chase
And all smiles ceased in a blink."

One who accepts death begins to live
One who rejects death begins to die
For the last passage is prickly packed;
Offers neither favor nor disfavor
Sees neither the hearer nor the speaker
The believer or nonbeliever
But listens for the haunting echoes
Of gravediggers as they clomp clods

There were plums of joy we plundered
Hunks of hurt we held to for far too long
Weights of anger we barely offloaded
Fears that spurred action or inaction
Glints of hope that nursed our losses

The unschooled desires steered
Rustic minds to twirl, the pure
Primeval furrows and fuel feuds;
The unsavory were lured
To pose ill- defined questions
To flatters in search of vain-glory.

Mortals devoid of hope,
Yearn for abiding grace,
Warm, embalming love
Gentle, serene care
The soft ray to light paths

The sane follow scurrilous scamps
To crave your presence and mercy.
Sheath us with your expanding shroud,
Lead us through the perilous straits
Till the radiant shore is reached and
Our yodeling clamps simply, imply close.

Joy is a Thought Away

When coming home is always a thought away
You unwaveringly reach for your dream.

Come, let us go you and I,
We, who left our shores of love and foes,
To labor in distant fields for meager sols
To fill our bellies and spent on paltry pallets.
Let's soothe our broken and sullen souls.

On the streets and half-deserted alleys
Courtiers in old and grubby garbs
Watch people debate recent foibles
That can be summed up as one folly.
Let's spread marmalade on our toasts.

We have come from far and not so far away
Places to share our ways of life only to
Witness tradition freeze time and lose
The vivid moments carved for posterity.
Let's count our winnings from yesteryear.

A singer ends an aria on the final note, and
Captures the floating echoes for a new song;
Clubs of ducks fly across the cobalt sky
To the drowned applause for a court jester
That failed to strum his three-strung guitar.
Let's go to the quiet and pleasant places.

For to have it told, is to know you have neither
The illusion to live in the bright light
Nor the wisdom to sway the intemperate
That is hooked on hearing your raspy voice;
The murmuring sentinel of hypocrisy;
Let's measure our lives with coffee spoons.

The earth creates fissures on monastic faces,
The tap-taps thud of sad and happy tales
Of man's brazen theft from his fellow man,
The ascendancy of greed over honest labor;
The dearth of wealth poised to honor thrift.
Let's parch the roosted trees needing cure.

Let's go and mark the means you seek;
The drive to swap war for illusive peace,
The differences formal or familiar;
The agonistics unsavory sway over order
The limited perceptions ending flawed justice
The consecrated of social ordeals
Set for hackneyed hacks like you and me.

Let's go and mend fences with the huddled masses;
Restore hope and fair play to their rightful places;
Places of thoughtful joy, and trust, and love;
That hold fear, and dread, and hate at bay
In a burrow safety for the unborn child, let us go.

Let's go to the home of the doomed and damned
The houses of misguided and discarded souls
Where compassion is shown by small deeds
And love is seen through the lens of kindness
Let's work with the cynics cycling the world.

Let's go, you and I, to palisade the temple;
Where regaled Desire holds sepulcher
And patiently waits on Vanity to confess
Her misdeeds to a skeptical court
That was fully aware of her chicanery.
Let us share laughter with the bereaved

Let's go when our time is done
For evil has its own beginning and end.
Good beginnings have good ends; and
Celebrate the beauty vested in you and me;
The kindness you feel, see and touch;
The joy filling your heart and mine with warmth;
For the rapture of love Bracey like
The coated seed is always a thought away.

Listen

It is in listening that we feel
The common bonds we share.

Listen to the silence in open spaces
The unspoken and the unheard
Voices of the damned and the free
Bridging breath with breathlessness.

Listen to the live voices that were stilled
And the stilled voices that were freed
The happy child dandled in loving arms
The tailwinds of the flying nightingale.

Listen to the plaintive cries of the child
Yearning to share its babbling thoughts
The broken-hearted tittering at the ebb
That sees only rile, flight and neglect.

Listen to the chants of orphaned children
The voices threading fear and hope
The calming voices gone hoarse
Foretelling things yet to come.

Listen to the silence of the soothing lyre
The bow heaving well-stringed cords
The last note on a music sheet
The echo ending a trail of long arias.

Listen to the silence of the servile heart
The joyful heart at the dawn of love
The bitter heart in the throes of grief
The hateful heart filled with vile.

Listen to the voices of divergent men
Mired in sin, and greed, and hate
The gentle heart filled with warmth
The caring soul reaching out to all.

Listen to the falconer's stealthy steps
Tracing the cries of the fleeing falcon
The tigress weeping for her lost cubs
The wind's indifference to signs of pain.

Listen to the wailing seagull
The cawing of the frisked macaw
The murmuring of the mermaid
Reminding one of the lost seafarer.

Listen to the anguish of the dead
Voices mired in pain and regret
The wailing voices of the bereaved
Meant to awaken the newly dead.

Listen to the poor cry plaintively
To the rich who sold their souls
To the goddess of greed and feed
The deaf man's voice lost to gifted gab.

Listen to social order craving justice
For the riddled body of the innocent
Stretched on a rack to be scavenged
By hangmen filled with vengeful rage.

Listen to the pattering drip drops;
The silent soaking drizzle
That fills ponds and streams with rain
The flood ripping nature with flare.

Listen to the harrowing wind
Blowing atop trees before uproot
The silence of the forest after
The sounds of the felled ceases.

Listen to the vespers sung at sunset
The enchanting voices of the robed
Joining heaven and earthly bodies
Reminding one of life and the afterlife.

For it is these voices that join you to me;
The drowned fauna in a palled pit
Fusing fear with hope, and peace;
The compassionate withered hand
Holding you to me, encircling all with love
Encircling all with mercy and forgiveness.

Poems from Macoma Beaches

Love Came For Me

The unchained melodies of life
Echo through generations.

Love came for me in the gap
When fear had vanquished
Hope and ringed umbra
Appears sweeter than nectar.

It draped me in its satin damask,
And pulled me from the pits
And I, like a tousled figure,
Followed as if possessed.

We passed the virgin greens
Where children in sashes play
The turrets of the church,
And did not hear the bell toll.

We passed the market hall,
The lit candle in office spaces,
The hamlet and the hovel,
The adults crouched at choices.

We passed the turret creek,
The busy taverns and Bacchus,
The vineyard and the cellar,
The drone of dunghill buzz.

We passed the fairy mother,
And the fairy father too,
Both appeared mired in magic
The seat of deception.

We saw the wondering fawn,
The hooded Adler slithering
Through a poke in the clod;
The king lying prostrate
The queen lost and quaint.

The pottery-bier close to
A man noosed from a tree
His reward of silver pieces
Scattered on the heedless soil.

We crossed the courtyard, and
Saw henchmen swinging axes
The digger buried in the pit
Meant for readied houses.

We saw the lay at the lee,
The pure and the sadist
At repast set for a heathen,
The chalice and the incense.

It pointed to the scripted
Entranced at the open sky
The scented wild flower
Drenching saved souls.

We passed the farmlands,
The smoke-stacked factories,
The sick homes and arid players,
The toiling hunchback of
Notre dame and the basilica.

We saw paupers and kings
In stiff and frozen poses.
The oceans and terrains torn
By arias of weeping willows,
The footmen hankering after grace.

We took a much needed pause,
A brief yet sudden
Just to rest, and recharge
But had to rejoin the track.

It looked at me and joyfully said:
"I am the beginning, middle and end
I am a master and a servant,
I am true, firm and strong,

I am kind, gentle and warm,
I accept not reject,
I trust and embrace
I am open and ever present,
I cherish all you are."

Lucumo

*Given virtuous support
Love will triumph over despair,
And hope over hate.*

Yet, once again I come to you the people of Entebbe
Who spend your lives in search of creeds, and greed
That knows no end. I come to jar your senses
With missive about the untimely death of Lucumo
Who enthralled us with unchained melodies
In arias, allegros and variations of pianissimos,
It must not be left un-mourned in the open pit of
The impervious pavement where it was felled,
Or left for the boos and kicks of wayward vagrants;
The goon that exchanges greetings with a warden
To tell it all at the rehearsal of Mozart's Requiem.

You must ring all beasts and men who heard its songs
To pay homage and eulogize the joy it brought
While unkempt warriors and vile cleric file by
The plumed Lucumo and debate merits of roasting it
To feed homeless prattlers in tight tatters
That sleep, and breed, and play in ravines
Close to abandoned and bordered posts.

It must be kept safe from shifty debaters
That script verses to incite social strife;
The crafty gibbers using mass suffering
To create converts and garner campaign funds;
Or goons subverting the rights of many to save skin;
The mourners in Shiva reciting suras to the insane;
The evil mind choosing gain over allegiance;
Ere Gentiles strut the stage set for coronation, and
The icy hand suddenly lowers the blade.

We clearly recall the wands you used to peg;
Our pillage and stack temporal portals; and
The nomad's probe to bridge pain;
The lustful Dust combing the haze
To save a restless soul at odds with itself.

Yea must we moan the red-breasted Lucumo,
Who stood at lowlands and highlands;
The blooming orchards; the forest greens and
The dust-dry Sahara and terrains in-between,
To enchant us with unchained melodies in mini scales
The sounds dappling the dawning day

We must trumpet its hymnals in octaves
To nobles' homes and slushy slums;
The faithful at the nave readied for a sermon;
The orphaned children and burdened hands,
To echo its love before a sexton breaks the earth.

Love Song of a Coward

The absence of bravery does not mean the presence of cowardice
Nor does naïveté turn to virtue on a whim.

Dare I dare or dare I not dare;
And, if I dared what would it be?
Dare I dot the 'I' seated in ice;
Remove the mote from my eye;
Cross the 'T' while sipping tea,
Or abandon caution to the wind?
　　　I will dare
　　　I will dare

Dare I present the perfect image
To a world trapped by perception
When imperfection is the norm;
Watch women come and go,
Or men caught by events of the time,
Say good-bye to friends and kin
They may see or not see again?
　　　I am true
　　　I am blue

Dare I disturb the "U" in urn
With my bratty prattle when others
Holding insightful thoughts
Rest at bay and only speak
When times are ripe and prime?
　　　I am here
　　　I adhere

Dare I spin thoughts in my head?
Sharpen the props I hold;
And tell only the truth;
Nothing but the truth,
Or hold on and say 'oomph'
To the narrowing chasm
Waiting for a better time to close?
　　　I will dare
　　　For it's rare

Dare I dare or dare I not dare
Present a well-constructed sign
To an undiscerning audience
With varied backgrounds;
Too scattered to bridge
The gap between truth and fiction;
Reflect on everything, all of it,
And, exclaim in a moment of despair,
I do not give a damn!
Or, hold my head high despite the odds
Confident of better days ahead.
  I will wait.
  I will faint.

Dare I seed my tested will?
A will tossed and tried in battle;
Defend the indefensible at the altar;
Flip a daft-lira from lunar,
Or, choose unknown outcome
As mantra, and hold on to it?
  Time will cease.
  Time will lease.

And, if I dared, what would it wroth
At the dawn when eyes are closed and
The senses numbed by
Reticence and false hope;
Or shall I sit still and stiff
Pivoted like a lodged marble
Sulking over what I could have been
While mocking the memoirs
Of a wayward coward;
Completely mired in self-doubt;
Gradually dying before my time;
Never striving to reach my dreams?
  I will live.
  I will give.

Ode to Solitude

Youth and moments have their places;
They belong to memory.
Age and waning lives
Share a single space
That belongs to mankind.

Oh! What a joy to live on the ticks of time,
Free from noisy streets and daily strife,
The visions of sonorous vespers
Hanging in empty monastic sanctum
With faith in life's offering
The delight in simple joys
The ease of self-assurance, and
The dare to bridge the chasm
Between the social and the solitary.

You firmly believe that
Living in the moment stiffens
Your resolve to share
Treasures of the soul with
Mystic givers and hallowed places.

To hold solitude in drowning din;
Remain open despite frightful
Moments of abject pain, and
Unclasp hinges holding
Peace at opened or closed spaces,
Like an uninspired conscript.

You hear lucid calm crating
Stillness between rippling waves;
The sea murmuring death and rebirth;
The core of cradling solitude
Holding humility in its hole.

You settled conflicts through stillness;
Joined mercy with forgiveness,
Temperance cuddling charity and
Whisked love from the wasteland
To share its beauty with rustic minds.

To be attached, you know, is to forgo
The parody of honest emotions;
The joys of living free and unfettered
The pleasures left for the eel,
The untarnished fullness saved
For persons who choose
Solitude with burning bodings over
Lives filled with brimming grime.

You affirm that children
Cheerfully assert and assist all;
They eagerly forgive and follow;
Observe to understand all,
Partake to embrace all;
Willing to forget and carry on
Without claiming full knowledge.

The care to measure love's expanse;
The honesty and depth of patience
And the opacity of compassion,
The hollowness of self-importance
Lost on inflated egos;
The weighty toll of discordant note;
The seasoned courage that knows
The source of its strength
Accepts the gift of being; and
The courage to live through the haze

In courts of divine justice
Conscience skips carnal law
To expose cruel and evil acts
Whether private or public, seen or unseen,
Heard or unheard;
To assert our common bond
The goodwill at the table
Where compassion is spread
Across varied lands
To free the wrongly accused or held
Into the arms of embracing solitude

Solemn is the wind that sails the scales.
Stiff is the mask that restores
The soul's desire to dispossess
So that it can cede peace
To the murmuring waterfall;
The buzzing bees at the beehive;
The crone sneaking by the coroner
To lead listeners to the loon;
The haunting chamber music
Buried deep in the soul of everyman;
The riddled fear of the wild expanse
Ever present, yet unseen;
The uncommon strength to hold on
Despite encircling chaos
Peace, quiet, still for all.

Of Freedom and Silence

Boundless freedom and frozen silence
The gap between action and inaction;
The gutted search for lasting values.

Thought and the study of language
Crime and the state of patronage
Man is ever moving, never static
Doing all he can not to be frantic.

Uncoiled waves like freed goose
Rattle doors until they are loose
But the gray and hungry agile bee
Looks for food with heartfelt glee.

Trotting foxes with keen eye sights
Do not engage in bawdy fights
But their antics appear only so-so
To a snail bent on escaping the snow.

Day creatures need nectar for sleep
Night creatures teach crickets to creep
But the barn owl filled with puffer
Likes to float with fluff and flutter.

Meals set for a family grounding
Assume the shape of the rounding
And when the dishes brim with meat
The cow ponders the need for retreat.

Nesting hens and nursing mothers
Have a thing in common with brothers;
Both care for weak and wily saddlers
Seeking refuge from roadside peddlers.

A droning, humming mosquito
Landed on my newly oiled pinto
To trade for blood and distemper
And fled before it lost its temper.

Readied bites and micro bits
Point me to crisps and mango pits,
Like spoonfuls of spices and onions
Cause one to question set opinions

Golden sunset and moonlit slumber
Remind me of the glowing umber
That glued my finger to the floor
When I tried to be a roaming Moor.

Daydreams like deep sleep dreams
Break through multi-layer reams
To focus all wondering aversions
On crooks used to steer aspersions.

But, summer heat and mating calls,
Steal silence from forest walls,
Like the cry of the newborn babes
Dousing desire with dribbling bribes.

From cradle to stuck out eaves
Sons and daughters review sleeves
When Lady Luck cracks a whip
To ease pain lodged in her hip.

Life's unbridled freedom,
Leads to a droned thralldom
As mediation brings change
To good fellows at the exchange.

Drip-drop tops the mounted taps
The kinds that keep you in wraps
Or bump you over the head
Would knock and drag you ahead.

You know the values defining you
The line separating me from you
The void joining all to none
The veil covering all and one.

Time informs us we quickly glean
Or, aspire to be really clean;
If food is served from a hot grill
And wealth is stowed in a dye till.

Yet, when the meal is readied for all
Siblings will show up on the call.
Justice will port mounded truth
Like barley surrounding rueful Ruth.

You stay fixed and rooted to the fold
Like time bridging youth with the old
You reign over the waves of the sea
Like an Augean oxen moored at the lea.

On Becoming an Adult

From dusk to dawn, or dawn to dusk,
The emptiness of our struggles span generations
To the meaningless bleat of a lost sheep
Our burdens heave our entrances,
We hug the hollowness lying between
The posts until we bow at the bar.

Soon, my Son and Daughter, you will be an adult,
And as you reach adulthood, you will learn
That time's moving cords string different tunes
But play similar harmonies for you and me.
You at the spring feast of life offerings;
And I, at the rehearsals of tired winter vespers.

You will learn laws presumed judicious and fair
Only dispense decisions and pseudo justice.
It bends with the moneyed-muse and sees
You as a vessel wittingly accepting its edict;
Ignorance of its intent will not count.
But mercy may counsel and forgive.
Its diktat is final, its grace is sparse.

Earn through labor, vision and honored sweat.
Be chary of yourself and employer's will.
Surrender first to self and your employer's will
Heed his words, and follow his rightful orders.
Perform your duties faithfully and well.
Let your errors guide your growth
Through reliance, patience and devotion.

Seek help from those more skilled than you
For time has pitched their minds'
Thoughts through roil, and toil, and foil.
Remember that all you know is
As a drop in the ocean of knowledge.
Be open to new thoughts and insights and
Thoughtfully assess all you sense and hear
For there are as many opinions as there are
Pathways to a destination; each with
Its seen and unseen perils and chances.
Look at the willow and learn from its ways;

It bends with the wind, the flood and the sun;
Yet, maintains its inner sway and strength.
Serve without surrendering your soul;
Meet your needs as you selflessly serve others.
Share your gains and enlist others to do the same.
Harm no one as you pursue your dreams.
Value those who are seen and heard
As you honor those who are unseen and unheard
For, in time, others will see the light
And follow the winding way from the lea.

Celebrate each life in your own.
Exchange good for evil, and good for good,
For we all suffer when our best is left to rot
And evil is freely traded.
Do not look for returns on your charity
Or count measure for measure,
That would be self-service.
There is no blessing in it.
Let your care be its own reward,
And, thank those who made it possible,
They are the truly deserving ones.

Listen to the unheard and the unspoken,
For the face of love is enlarged
When we affirm the soul through compassionate
Listening, forbearance, and steadfast acceptance.

Live in peace with yourself and inner light.
Give love to those who embrace it from you,
And forgive those who wrong you
For it is through care and forgiveness that
Our world is renewed and strengthened.

Resist calumny and shameful acts
That hurt your home and places of service.
Speak your truth simply and quietly;
Recognize the difference and sameness of
The people you see or encounter
For they share in the right to be here.

Be judicious in your benevolence and weary
Of persons that are eager to please
For they often carry daggers in sheaths
And hearts of villainy, envy or greed;
They maim without care and kill without mercy.

Reject guile offerings in glitzy wraps.
Time will beam its grace on your stance
For others to see the path you carved.
Pace yourself, and protect your life,
For life is a precious gift worth preserving.
Be content with your station in life
Even as you look deeply into your soul and
Empty it of greed, envy, hate, and malice
To celebrate each man's life in your own
And affirm your oneness with all beings.

Rejoice in the small and big moments
As life peels its petals of hope and loss
And time heals grief, hurts, and pain
For brooding ties you to the past,
While the present passes unspent into the infinite.

Be cheerful as you lie in the valley of life,
For life's sudden twists are laced
With boundless beauty, joy and laughter;
And remember, always remember, my dear,
There is a place you are always loved.

Passing the Torch

Saying goodbye is never
Easy even in good times
When all is well and the
Body is aligned with the soul.

You came to visit on my outbound journey
And decided to stay to join
The past with the future and
Ruefully ignored the direly present;
The tolling of the bell urging me
To bid adieu and pass on
The torch to you and
Cross the bar at the appointed hour
To meet faces of yesteryear,
And ready for faces yet to dawn.

Did you come to coach yourself of
Where to begin your inward journey,
Or, having begun, build a frame
To guide your destiny
When the time comes for your soul
To fleche the carnal divide
Which egged the falconer to still the falcon, and
The magpie to crack the obelisk window
With a sigh readied for the newly widowed?

You and I shared sadness and joys together,
Drifted apart and came together.
We saw the births and deaths of children;
The dour events that mark our times;
The travails of countries and cultures
As they transit chasms of emptiness
To transform despair into ideal beauty,
And we were amazed.

We soared on the wings of solitude,
Floated joyfully into the firmament,
To hear murmuring mallards
And clacking albatrosses,
And thought they sang to us.

We bowed to kiss Bacchus' brow
But, stopped before we debased ourselves
At the orgiastic altar where ecstasy
Rules like pretense and true love is
Humbled or blighted for all to see.

I was beached alone
And must leave alone
Without dare or dread
On the hour of the striking toll
To join peace within with peace without;
And return earth-to-earth; dust-to-dust;
Ash to ash;
The creature to its Creator;
And end the vertigo that
Deemed me as a means.

Time abates all pain and desires;
Faith endures all pain and pining;
Duty commands attention
Even as the coo-coo coos requiems
To soothe jilted lovers mired in self-pity.

The seasons move at their rhythms;
The sired leaves float into their wintry beds
To nourish mother earth for the planting.
The bouncing rabbit burrows for warmth;
The soaring sparrow splices the wind
Or floats and flutters the flat and highlands
To settle on treetops or the bog.

You lost what you used to be
To ready the self for what it has to be;
But held on to your soul,
The center of your faith and being

To fend off the ineffable,
So that your spirit can ascend to
Enchanted places filled with
Fragrance and mystic chants
To clarion a new day
Filled with kindness and renewals.

Pendjari Park

Quietude is as welcome to an abbess
As chaos is to the restless mind.

The pond stood still in the whipping wind
The pond stood sentry at the entrance of time
Time passed through space into the infinite
The formless shadows of a moonless night
The stars and the frozen sky cease to matter.
      Quiet is the hour
      Silent is the moment.

Raindrops flooded the delta and ceased,
The hoopoe oop-ooped and flew away
The angels warned of what was to come
Lucifer showed us the way to wealth
And we followed it with all speed.
      Grant us your patience
      Grant us your wisdom.

The clumsy double-horned hippo trapped
The toad continually croaked a dirge at
Odd hours to jar silence from its slumber
The hogget hobbled on its heels at Pendjari
The piglet picked its way through the gyro.
      Free us from debt
      Free us from envy.

The white cuckoo borrowed the beaver's nest
The Pel's Fishing–owl snatched a pike in its talon
The Black mamba slinked from the scorpion
The mooing cow closed in on a dove's croon
The Roan Antelope kept vigil over the vale.
      Dour is the hour
      Dire is the moment.

Torrential rains pattered the savanna forest
The winds carried dust across the open Sahara
The Wasp Spider weaved its silver web by day
The sly skunk stayed burrowed by night, and
The woodland Kingfisher dared one and all
To mark the making and breaking of life.

> *Protect us from wars*
> *Protect us from evil.*

The crowned crane crawled to the honey badger
The masked weaver sought refuge beneath rocks
The pika searched for plankton near the waterfall
The hunter neither strung nor shot his arrow
The haunted never pardoned or inspired fear.
> *Keep us humble*
> *Keep us safe.*

The rising sun shortened the dawning shadow
The falling sun lengthened the dusking shadow
They exchanged greetings in a formless haze
They showered love on unlovable creatures.
> *Give us your blessings*
> *Forgive us our debts.*

The pulses pass never to return;
The tired souls become clumpy sods
The bottle and the seasoned wine
Brewed from grapes of peace and war
Cast long silhouettes on the living dead.
> *Grant us your Vision*
> *Grant us your Peace.*

Reflections

Nature and time join hands
To churn our bodies from vibrancy into decay
But, the brave are ever ready for the
Summon to the post.

As I look at the reflection of my face,
The furrowed brow and graying eyelids;
The thinning hair and receding hairline
The sallow cheeks and felled teeth; I see
The death of youthful intemperance on
The last step of a closing gyre, clasping
Tallow-candle at the altar of Elysium
The victor-victim of vacuous times.

I hear frayed flakes of recondite leaves,
The budding buds and tweaked twigs
The autumn gales combing the roost
For writhed fruits for fire ants that
Flick and glint and know not why.

A gathering of families and friends
Tell stories to teach and amuse
The lives at hand before their prime;
The silent breathing of the hermit
That eases quietly into the infinite;
The moving melee in sundry milieus
That melts away with the passing, and
The heedless merriment of Joy Street
Bringing bliss to one and all.

I spot grieving parents wailing over tots,
The sash padded mats and dribble spits;
The enchanting friends and passers-by,
The full life vaulted to feed miasma,
And the gains greed garners
To trade freedom for dependence;
The spitting wobblers scaling friable life;
The radiant sun burning the soft mist,
To birth brilliant poses for the day.

I see Shame awaking cynics
To spread their wings and
Soar eagle-like into the firmament;
The elliptically fathomable, yet unheard;
The unsteady steps of toddling children
The loss of innocence waiting in the wings.

I picture youth ardently chasing
Reflections of a tapering mirage.
The sleepless hours spent fancy-free
On ideas that grow to nothingness
The withered prune hanging down
A sapless tree defying
Pleasures tied to time and the tidal waves.

I hear discordant cries of the servile scum,
The deserted and downtrodden, eking misery
To ease the weighty yoke of their lot;
The unbridled justice time endows
The equipoise pitting fact against fiction,
Accepting ugly ogres as urbanely real,
The cheap-side chimp in sanguine rattrap.

I spy the parks Mama and Papa used to tread,
I skip over the glinting puddles;
The follies of moony days and buzzing flies,
The thick grown grass scaring kids and
The cultured fear taming all and sundry.

I think of gestures made to give pleasures,
The strung arrow aimed at lousy louses,
The darts that twit and twitter, and
The effectual collapse of ill-built plays.

I recount the lost and unseen guests who
Wore plated pants without intending to;
The isolated dragged to cross
The chasm that inspires us to borrow friends
At crowded and strange places;
The blank talks made to amuse with follies
And the time spent to reap nothingness.

I remember the muse changed to evil,
The burdened daring to live and flourish
Instruction in arrogance meant
To support miscreants who believe:
"Nostalgia is Future's worse enemy."
Oh, how sweet it is to carve a space in time,
To dream over joyful moments I had or
Make revisions that are true and thorough.
The chosen path leading to the desired end;
The end meant to unveil its being,
The ignoble end unaware of its poor roots,
The cowered Truth at the altar of Hope.

Oh, how sweet it is to carve a space in time,
To ponder the errors I made,
Make revisions that truly serve their goal;
See foggy future totally defogged;
The end for one fully set;
The noble soul rightly hailing its genesis,
Porting Truth to the altar of Conscience.

I regret the small things I could have done
To ease another's pain and did not do;
The big things that turned into littleness,
The unresolved conflicts left in rods to rot,
The love of fellows pinned to the rack;
The elongated shadow forgiveness
Casts to ease endless pain, and
The breadth's cry for fitting exit,
As the requiem ushers me atop a gyring pile.

Sunset and evening fall bring laborer to an end.
Time closes the chapter for one and all;
The earth oozes heat to cool its core.
The trees whine to end a stressful day,
The pebbles tumble and fall; and
The busy ant churns sod for the howling wind
To haul across the immense openness,
Like grains of thoughtless landforms
Swatting swallows in endless waves.
A caller yells, "You almost reached yesterday
To mend fences with those you wronged."

I close my eyes to rapturous echoes,
Ringing for all that dare to hear
Stories of joy and genuine friendships;
Unfettered love and endless passions;
Journeys of warmth, beauty, and joy,
The yoked slave and the brash master
Readying oakum to plug galley meant
To ferry peace and love to all peoples.
The forlorn moments of the fatally faint,
Feigning death is better than endless pain.
That HOPE is tethered to good deeds; and
Vision inspires faith to say
With crystal clarity: "What a ride! What a life!"

Remembrance

Passages of yesteryear and
Passages from the present
Portend to a future in the
Present and a present of the past.

Childbirth and child death
The passage of time and
The capture of time;
Time past, which once stood for
Time in the future;
The passage of time in seamless flow
Till it crosses the hourly bar
And everything ceases to matter.

We gathered as a people ready for
Action and doubtful of what to do
About our reasons for being or reactions.
The night long vigils spent
Pouring over listless lives at
Underpasses or overpasses;
With common and uncommon purpose;
At scheduled and unscheduled hours
To remind us of time past
And time future and what we did
Or could have done while time present
Flies into the infinite, never to return.

We talked of trendsetters that
Carved new cultural paths and
Transformed social orders;
Freedom seekers that embrace,
The birth conscionable governance
Watched their efforts fizzle at the shore.

Between the summer of content,
And the winter of discontent;
Between the will to do good
And the compassion that uplifts all

The drive to deed evil for evil;
The cynical evil that deflates all,
We shared verses of convictions,
When we played at the public park
And used wood-carved trowel
To fill our pails with pebbles
Which we emptied and refilled;
With help from tiny toddling hands,
And teens committed to good causes.

You shared tales of your travels
To different lands and peoples
Strange and novel ways of being;
Foods that looked much the same
And had different taste or smell;
Rustic places and opal palaces,
The virgin forest filled with surprises;
The dirge to baneful memories
The chime to blissful memories
Pealing to affirm our sameness.

You defended the racked laws
Elitists passed to suppress
The poor and the dim-witted;
The ruthless wrecking of the weak and
Einstein's order of the universe
Pitted against the pastoral verses,
And deeded your findings to posterity.

You re-examined the pillars of virtues
And, oh, what a re-examination, and
Found a trove of vices and devices
Continually struggling for definitions
That enjoin the raying sun
To expose subtle deception
Or battled thought of encircling bends
That molded our views.

You recalled your rush to possess
And trust in faith and dispossession
The abyss of sullen disdain and
The lost of serenity; a sense of emptiness
And the fixes of forded knowledge,
The tattletale peeling the layers apart
To expose the narrow gap between
The thoughtful dote and the thoughtless sage.
The dearth of a desolate mind
Hardly hankering to reach truth.

Family, you said, came in varied shapes
And fain to share the presents they have
With one and all in close spaces
At expected and unexpected places
And at times with a ready world
In open embraces at hallowed places.

Children, you said were gifted
To grace our path and renew growth,
To drink in nature's scattered beauty;
The professed hope and fear
That affirms our purpose and dispassion.

Forgiveness, you said was the swirling wind
Of inverted kindness that
Filled our sail for life's journey
And steered our soul to soar
Into the large expanse of the sky.

Compassion, you extolled, stoked
The flames of intemperate desire
To usher us into the urn-filled temple
Where our souls clasped at the mantle
Of human loyalty
Joined you to me, and one to all.

Hate, I heard you say, was
The evil within that ate
The soul like canker and
 Defiles us with maggots;
A poverty of the spirit
That distorted and destroyed
Anything it saw and touched.

Wars, you said, were waged by
Weak thoughtless leaders
Who had lost their moral compass
And came to believe that
Force was the only true answer
Until statesmen come to the fore
And society sees a different option.

Peace, you said, birthed inner serenity,
It honored everyman's lot,
Rejected evil as a rational;
The contentment of the unfettered self
And the ascendancy of care over evil.

Love, I remember you hail
Was chase to those who accept its ways;
It's ever patient and never condemning.
It's ever affirming and never disdaining.
It's ever embracing and never disbanding.
It's ever fertile and never vapid.
And, you, my dear, are my love!

Life, you said, was filled with
Choices made and choices discarded,
Visions of faith and revisions by design
That manfully enjoined you
To free your soul from solitude and
Returned you to the fiestas of humanity;
The plants and the animals that
Nurture and amuse;
The bountiful earth that celebrates

Time in open or closed spaces;
The offerings shared with you,
The humility to accept the offerings made to you.

Rings and Squares

We hear and do not heed
We heed and do not share
The jubilant voices
The sad afflicted soul
The divide between action and thought
The thought joined to action
The trap confounding decisions.

Lives have been gained,
Lives have been lost,
But to what end is life's gain
Or the measure of life lost
When life that is fully unlived,
Floats freely like the wind.

The spindle of the carousel
Carries children through space
Like the threading of a needle;
One is manmade,
The other belongs to nature;
Both know neither beginning
Nor how they will end
For in the middle of life
There is dread,
And in the eye of dread
There is a new beginning,
The known and the unknowable,
The visible and the invisible
Holding the mystery of life
That appears open and closed;
The clear and the murky
Visions and revisions
That do not flex or deny
Time tested truths
But expire without a trace
Like the etherized vapor
Yearning to avoid pain,
But eager to embrace
Fantasies that feed life.

For when eyes are closed
And the ears can barely hear,
The day begins anew;
The dew-drenched leaves
Guide the unsure steps
Of the lonely traveler
At the fork in the road
To unfurl the gripping vice
Of retreat and perseverance
To pierce the impenetrate veil.

The desire to hold,
The fear of novelty,
Hope in frightening guises;
The simple and complex stances;
Homes that are full or barren
Join hands at the center
And break bread at a drawbridge;
Unhinge the chains that bind
To begin life anew
And let spirits freed
From bondage of care;
Live with renewed vigor
At the beginning of circles
Or the end of rings,
That keep appointed hours
For well and ill-defined reasons.

Stanley Sackeyfio

Scansions of Respect

The closed and opened spaces
That clouds and silent voices fill
Only partly define who we are; not all we could be.

Cleaved from a different hew
Yet part of you and everyman
At times paltry and primitive
At times envious and vain;
The wicked and the kind;
You, in your mighty mansion are
Barred from the bracken barrios;
The cultures that instruct and mold
The visions that inspire love and hate,
The urge to map schema into
A tapestry that binds and guides.

I rent a robe into two for us to share;
One for you, and the other for me
For we bow to the ways of our fathers;
The joining of our present to the past, and
The yearning for a place to empty our pain
So our hearts can heal to free our souls.

Yet, everywhere the silence of the tomb
Haunts you and me; love quavers
Discordant calls to whip the air
And waken us to the hyena's dirge;
The yodeling of the midnight fox, and
The ache of the orphaned at dusk
Who ditched love and prudence
When he needed them most
As truth bowed to hate and not love
And imams and rabies hatched a plan
To kill innocence and hold hope at bay.

We learned to hate and not look for love,
We dared to leave and not die to hold,
We clipped the bond and not sacked the scum
The Light ceased to self-portray
And the aegis of disdain clouded the land.

But when the radiant colors of Respect
Greet us at dawn with smiles
We grin from ear to ear like daisies
And ask why we did not share its
Virtues with friends and strangers
Or the neighbor who came to our aid
When Grace was gaunt and gritty.

The effusiveness of its simplicity,
The lift of its noble expressage
Assailing homebound vessels;
Returning one to all and all for one.
Life in the shadow of its control;
The difference severing none;
The thoughtful hearts nurturing love
At unexpected times and places
The hidden treasures in open places
The respect denied to self and all
The respect given to one and all.

Shadows of our Past

A ghost is a thing of imagination
Yet, despite its illusion, man is haunted by its specter.

I do not desire to know your lineage
The borrowed colors of Ebonics or chicanics
The depth of your dispassion, or passion
For what you are disdains my people.
I do not share your vision or values.
But desire to watch you feast on gruel
Only your constitution can command.

I scorn your presence at the kitchen counter;
Playing or polling with you
For the soot floating from your soul
Soils the sweetness of the air I breathe.

I renounce your tales of rejections, and
The violations of law and commerce to
Benefit my kind. Schooled in caution,
I remain politic, polite and coy at
Bending the rules to serve my whim,
Using fine talk to enforce orders
Geared to exact conformity to my will, and
Your metalloid soul to my caprice.

I resent the roots of your numbed norms,
The gatherings used to spread messages,
And sway congregations that clap in unison,
To discordant tunes in virulent quartets.

You come from the shantytowns, in tatters
The ragged colors of wide and strange places
To grub and scrub and serve at my ward and
Homes built on the servile backs of your fathers.
I dart hateful arrows at the core of your soul.
Yet, you remain resolute in love of duty,
And heartily smile for a hireling.
So that you may claim crumbs from my table;
And cower for my "kindness";
Only to return to my winter bed
When time and illness writhed my body.

Yet, as youth, when blood was warm
And life was rife and zestfully blooming,
I damned the sweat of our parentage;
The childhood times of fun and play
The toddler's trot and the paddy cakes
The xystus, open parks and in hidden valleys.
I conjured you as a foe fit for tweaking
To meet the deontology of my senses.

Is it your steeled spirit that keeps you aloft?
Or, has etherified time numbed your senses
To the slow smoldering moss
Or have the petals of my petty shame
And attempts at loving you
Palled the likeness of our kin
To cast us in a play whose actors
Mimic the shadows of our past?

The Adventurer

To love is not easily confused;
To hate is not truly admired;
The search for meaning and
The acceptance of one and all.

In the morning as I left home
I heard seafarers and Sacked-friars
Talking of war and peace,
The efforts made to reach either end;
The need for all forms of freedom;
And the shatter of serfdom.

Traders trekked on camelbacks
For spoil and pitch for converts
The pirates hunted for loot;
The runs made to load bootie
The jute bags for Jubilee.

A melee of men scratched
For gold with good measure
Clear spices for binding
The cloves cleaved with glee
And the land is left to ponder
Why it was easy to plunder.

A sickle swung to harvest
Labor's summer toil fills silos
The remnants feed flamingos
The noble hearts jot missives
On tablets to nunnery abbes
 Extolling virtues of humility.

The traveler rambled and babbled
About faith in the new-found world
The distrust of what is left to hold
The drilled nail in a perfect finger
Dripping blood, sapped with vinegar.

He mentioned a carpenter at his shop,
Telling of how to splinter boards
Or turn bows into sharp arrows;
The tooter's dash for the scimitar
And Judas' purse spread on the tar.

Time will pass and time will come,
To mark wars and fogged peace
The doves of peace, the hawks of war
The agent's suffer for war victors
The debate held with senseless actors

He praised the psalmist's take on sura
The raja's combing Sumatra
For an imam reading a Bible verse
And claiming victory for converts.

Words meant to mould and teach
Beyond one; the love given to each
By those loving through daily turns
Urging us to strew ashes from urns.

He said he met a man in Timbuktu
Unaware of the ballerina's tutu
So, he spent days and long nights
Telling stories about human rights.

He arrived in the city of Rotterdam
To dredge the Rotte river for a ram
But soon found the hype unsalable
To coxswains that reject the incapable.

He journeyed to the Australian jungle
In search through a wide lens angle
But walked away with an Aborigine
Set on living outside every hegemony.

He sailed to the coast of Easter Island
With aku-aku to comb a nearby land
For treasures that were lost or hidden
Only to hear dreary noises from a den.

He walked the long halls of Taj-mahal
To meet the wife who inspired it all
And sat down for a much needed rest
At the tomb with an unguarded crest.

He looked over the leaning Pisa
And discussed its uses with Elisa
Just when the sun ray on a grotto
To instruct gamblers to play lotto.

He told tales that were wholesome
Of men who killed to save a Kingdom
The God and Allah that loves us all
And efforts made to avoid a great fall.

He saw human flaws in river flows
The lifeline that glints and glows
The spirits that guide us to the shores
The sailors snaking through the Azores.

He arrived home worn and tired
To share his tales with the retired
And found they were too busy
To hear stories told for the cozy.

The Deserted City

Desertion is a thought in the making
Redemption is an action found on faith.

Let's go, you and I, let us go
Let us go to the city's sanctum
Of dimmed and bright lights
Lights meant to trail and invite
Let's go after our work is done, and
The day is spent for you and me, and
All the others that toiled at
The old and not so old mills,
With passion and dispassion
Till the bell tolled and
Another day's work is ended
Let us go!

Let's snake through
The bayous and wastelands;
The eddish kirks and eddied dens;
The taste of synod sauternes,
And visit places called homes;
That are not so homey
The abode of the broken;
The pillaged and bilked
That lost their dreams
To the raging fire
That could not read
The signs of war or want
Let's go!

Let us steer to the seats
Tucked near the city streets and
Watch hurried-time ease
Her huddled masses of
The languid and deserted;
Men in fancy suits and flying cravats
Daffy-cuffed and fancy-fitted
With burnooses and turbans
Claptrap heels and duffle bags
Hop trails and trains to known
And unknown destinations

Till noon-cast shadows fall
And the pall mulls all
Let us go!

Let's go and read the faces
The bare and buried faces
Walled or void of secrets
Faces of hope and joy;
Of pain and despair
Faces that are bon and not bonhomie
Faces veiled for you and me
The marketer and the marketed
The cheater and the cheated
The friendly, drab and dreary,
Caustic but not rustic
Let us go, you and I,
Let us go!

Let's mark men and women
In shaded garbs of green and gray
Red, blue and yellow too
Saris and caftan, sarong and burqa,
The covered and dust-dry hair;
Painted lips and bindi faces,
The women of high and low classes
The high and low standards
The suave and the simple
Let us go watch them
Tote bags, purses and umbrellas
Zigzag from boardroom to rooms
Which are neither boarded nor bound
Journey to homes of one or more
Meant for none or more
Let us go!

Let's look at the pale glasses
The clear and open displays
Showing garbed mannequins
The chiefs carried in palanquins
The kinds meant to move purchase
By the rich of Wall Street
And the poor of Main Street
The passer-by on a daily walk

That only cares for firm steps
And the infirm search for leaps
Let us go!

Let's tramp the damp hotels
Of Cheap-side streets;
The smoke-filled taverns
Reeking of cancer sticks
Where regaled Bacchus and
Rankly kegs hold sway over
The drink-dipped faces
Swooned over barstool stallions;
The tipper-dipped and tipsy
That toast tiffs to wins or losses
Hashed and unrehearsed thoughts;
Till nothing is left to pun or ponder
But giddy heads awaiting shame
Let us go!

Let's bridge the broken ridge
Left for the dead and the dying
Rodents-riddled, and dearth-darned
The dislodged and homeless
Tight-fitted and loose-Sida clothes;
Half-torn, and half -patched-shoes;
Knitted hair and vacant eyes;
The half–crushed men and women,
The discarded and social scum;
The outcasts of a rich society
The wealthy of a poor society
The seer and withered masses
Standing sentry at street corners
Ready to tease tithes, one and all,
Let us go!

Let us view the gap between
The people of difference or sameness
Gamble and babble for change
As we ramble and bramble about
The reef knots and juggernauts,
The simple travelers in carriages;
Knighted infants in pulled wagons
Pained and anguished parents

Wringing hands in disbelief over
The changing fortune for seers
In the last lapse of life, and
The lot of generation yet to come
Let us go!

Let's soothe the toddling tattler's pain
The garb of morphed innocence
Growing minds in growing bodies;
Carped for "love" and "hate"
And emotions in-between
Until care comes to all
Desirous to mend broken spirits and
Restore joyful smiles to its rightful abode.
Let us go!

Let us hug the Brackenridge;
To watch the setting sun exchange
Glances with the moon, and
Bow below the line to relight
Deserted lives and dreamy heads;
The dawn of a new circle
Wresting life from dusk
Bidding the rooster to clarion
Easeful birth and renewal;
Let's go, you and I,
To meet the readied faces that
Slickly fuse the line between war and peace.
Let us join celebrants at the gateway of time;
Let us go!

The Dew

Things of beauty, gentleness and grace
Often leave without a trace.

The haze came early in the morning
And dropped damp dreary dew
Filled with soft, drizzly water
On my porch, and flower-pots.

It drenched my necklace and necktie
The red, satin sheet and fine linen
The locked socks and the frocks
Hanging on the sisal laundry line.

It doused the raging, smoldering fire
Burning the fields and the fauna
Manmade homes and open pits
It swooned by the rocks and locks
And eased by the mast and outpost.

It bogged graded gravel and soil
It soaked tree tops and mountain tops
The ponds and the honey pots
To set the bee abuzz through the air.

It draped the flowers in sweetness
The growing buds in fullness
Dampened the hot, dry, steamy air
And avidly birthed coolness

It climbed the ice-cap of Everest
To visit the air that never rests
Seesawed with the briny sea
The rough, bouncy, wavy waves
The whale, the dolphin and the elf.

It nuzzled my window panes
To awaken my dulled senses
Just like the sun spires darkness and
Tenderly said, "Good morning Sunshine,"

To the hearing of the shrubberies
And left without a trace.

The Fair Season

Our fortunes change with time's
Tick tocks to spin its axis.

Fall leaves and feathered beds
Seared leaves and sired lives
May the seasons guide the cycle
Through the tumid river
For these are the times when the
Day shortens and we measure
What we did, or did not do;
The days to finish what we could
Before we join the silent shadows
And our voices are drowned.

Winter coats the temperate zones with
Cold, and snow, and sleet and ice,
Snowstorms coat the tundra,
The peak of Everest with icicles;
The ground hog burrows deeper, and
The owl ceases to whoo or whisper.
But over the plains of mother Africa
The fiery winds ferry Sahara's
Reddish sand atop roosted trees
To seed rain across the pond.

Women in woven mittens mix muslin
For haggard men hewing winter wood;
The yaks, and the fobs are felled.
Teens talk of tasks stretched to growl
The trapped heat and bolted doors;
The frosted red-nosed Reindeer
Cress-crossing frozen prairies to hide
Toys under the amaryllis for nimble hands.
But, in mother Africa the children have only
The red dust to heed, and greet, and feed.

Spring bloom and zestful zithers,
Fill the roosted branches with life.
The geese trek to the amber trees,
The full-plumed monarch butterfly
Returns to the breeding foothills
Of Capistrano to begin life anew.

The snow-capped mountains melt;
The hunter slays the hunted, and
The bovine beaver dams the bog
With reeds, and weeds, and seeds, and
Knows not why the charge.
The magpie, the finch, and the falcon
Refuge in the sprouting trees
Awaken the python and the bony bear,
With "wocks,""beeps,"and "kak-kaks."
Lovers warmly welcome,
The emerging warm days.

Summer's heat and the buzzing flies
The waves joining heat to the wasteland
The tabled freshness from the land, and
The bounces bobbing rabbit in its robe
Brings delight to starved predators.
But, in mother Africa the children
Have no seeds to plant or harvest.

The fleeting air wags twirling kites
That float, and dive and wane.
The fog of romance clears
The heads of the newlyweds who
Were so much in love to view
The tasks that lie ahead
For one and both in tethered times.
But, in mother Africa, the sea eats
The coastline and the plankton too.

Friends gather in shaded trees
To exchange views meant for threes
Children giggle over winter goblins and
Renew friendships the winter frayed.
The famished owl bobs out to hoot, or
Spy squirrels scalp nuts for supper.

The frail fawns forage for feed or buffer
While the gray billed swallows exchange
Greetings with the hanging bats
And plans their moves for the coming days
Over objections of the brown-haired robin
That twits below the arch of the birch tree.
But, in mother Africa, the weathered trees
Are bare of fruits for man or beast.

Full-bloomed flowers scent the air with
Sweet smells for the buzzing bees to feed.
The bush blue butterfly asked a supine spider:
"What to do with the dead and the living?"
"Go ask the seasons, for I do not know," it replied.
"And neither do I," added a sagacious imp.

The Junction

At the point where four roads meet
You debate from whence you came
And whither to reach for
Inner peace or contentment.

Dilemmas redefined you in all phases of life
Yet you drank life to the lees, and
Wonder at the shores of every clime,
Whether time is ripe for you to distil
Your thoughts and present them to an audience
Assembled on the precept of self-discovery.

You bend ideas to fit known and notions
Active experimenters and creative artists
To construct a perfect mantra
That is neither better nor worse,
For would-be leaders and followers.
You looked to skeptics to convince idealists
About carving order from disorder
To stitch tapestry of social harmony.

Daylight and sunset direct sophists
To accept the transience of knowledge
Being, nothingness, and allness;
Value inspiring human virtues
Bridge the gap between purpose and change;
The ants gradual churning of the soil;
The uncertain outcome of labor, and
Capture dreams lost to fear.

Nomads seek shelter for rest at dawn
After roving the vast and dusty wasteland
Just when nannies and nuns assemble to care
For discarded infants and haggard hacks
Concealing wounded hearts from the fold
When they learnt the world likens their
Contributions to ones by fallen heroes
Whose value rose only after their passing

The riddles of consensus formation
Holds Justice in one hand and
The Crucifix of social morality in the other
As faiths debated science inventions.

The clap-trap, trap-clap of a marching soldier
Separates silence from its tranquil repose
The hollow tree echoes the owl's eerie hoots
The sounds of the hunter's gun hollows
Against the solemn requiem sung
For the sorrowful piping Gray Horn bill;
The shaggy rat rants at the vulture
Retired atop a dry and barren tree
Awaiting the return, the dawning of day
When it would scavenge the remains
Of kills left in the wake of destruction.
Clay-to-clay; ash-to-ash, earth-to-earth;
The promises kept and the hopes dashed.

Dreams of an insipid socialist;
Dreams of an idealist believing in
Value vested in each species that
Ignore markings life leaves in its wake.
A rush to hear the inner harmony;
The unheard humming by the deaf;
And the yawns fetuses make in wombs.

Protagonists vigorously debate
The lot of the victims of natural disaster;
The plights affecting people
In faraway lands they had never seen,
Or met and only partially understood;
The cultures that divide and unite,
The home and family we seek
At affordable prices in unaffordable places!

The trumpeter cannot hear triumphs
Or the hermit the forest's howl
For both are engaged with
The muse and the chambermaid in
New creations and planned destructions;
The comatose and the living
Whose struggle for contentment

Only manage to recapture pseudo life
At a junction where visions and astrolabes
Are revisited and soon revised
Like heliographs moored to quicksand.

The Kalahari Desert

*It is more honorable to accept wisdom later in life
Than to live in continuous folly.*

The clouds agreed with the lively seasons
To hide Namib in the den of goddess Naiad,
And secure a narrow corner of the earth
Below the ashen dome of the Kalahari.

The brine-drenched otter dithers
At the edge of the jiggered rock
To utter a harsh ultimatum
To the knackered jackal strutting to
The wild roaring waves of the Atlantic.

The green gecko growls at the black raven;
The silver-crowned vulture slavers over dross;
The drenched ghoul dragon prowls
The sandy expanse for the fleeing ostrich.

Thoughts without form like empty context
Breathe through the veins of soulless men
Readied atop a sand-baked pyre, and
No caring hands to soothe elfin children
Lying on the lap of udder-less mothers.

The senseless simoom rolls to suffocate
Every life that lies in its path;
The long-tailed scorpion crawls across
The sand dunes to duel the sidewinder snake
At the billabong of Okavango with
The hard-shelled Dung Beetle as onlooker.

Gone are the days when hunters foiled death
Gone are the days when plankton meant life
And desert beasts trotted the tumid Delta
At discrete hours to play, rap, or bathe.

Gone are the seasons when gargoyles filled
The drill trekking down the gyred gutters
Onto the gray granite rock of covert caverns
And the Elf Owl shamed the bullfrog into silence.

Damned are the empty souls
That willed half-built statues
As legatees to their heir;
The simple, candid infant
That lives in one and all.

Long is the wait when Hope's path is
Strewed with gloom and despair;
Dread is the hour when life is
Left in the care of executioners.

Lost is the dirge when breadth bows to death,
And hemlock, drank in drams, tastes sweeter
Than the sweetest wine toasted to celebrate
The untimely end of a long laboring day.

Silent is the echo when the curtain falls and
The beauty of the Kalahari ceases to be.
Mute is the muse when
The note fades into the infinite, and
The dappled leaves cease to cleave.
Do I wake or drown?

The Leaf

The end was in the beginning
And the cycle held on to its endless journey.

The leaf floats on the waters
And careens the tumid currents
Even as life shoulders all
And ferries foes to fertile lands

The leaf wears its stipules
Around its shoulders like a cloak
The budding and the birth of spring
The toddling steps and the genesis
The weight of the world in ring

The vein and the yellow leaf
Seared between life and lifelessness
Dreading return to the rutted earth
From whence it sprang like a star
Trapped between form and avatar

The welted willow reef
Dry and dusty, moss and musty
Creasing across the iridescent sky
Beckoning the unheeding wind
To hoist it over the raging inferno
Fizzing through fissures in the earth

The synched, dark leaf,
The prickly, paisley leaf,
The speckled, green leaf,
The sickened, spotted leaf
Condyle like a coiled bone
Snaking the sinews of grief

Totem tows its labyrinth
The veins, blade and petiole
And joins it to the stem of life

The source of its strength;
Social hues in a benign noose
Rush to coat evil with the good

Freed of time, arrested in space
The beginning and the end
Are oft wrapped in seamless flow
The path to eternal peace floats
On the unsure voices of the known
Faith embraces the unknown
And the leaf is tested at the core.

The Otter

Awash, awash, I am ready to play
And which sod is ideal for molding
For I have play on my mind and not ready for a fray.

When all is said and thought done
Things may still be left undone
But one thing that is always true
Is the line written to express rue.

For after the rain the cloud clears
And the debtor remains in arrears
The creeks fill with rain water
The tasks are left till much later.

A farmer with ten mouths to feed
Weighs tithes with a sense of greed
And as the soil begins to recede
He ponders what he has to concede.

A banker is forced to bow and greet
Warriors who fled from the fleet
To families that are from the fiord
That closed ranks into one accord

We all, all spend much, too much
Time on trash that turns into mulch
Or postpone actions till the morrow
When cultured debtors can borrow

But, the osprey desirous to be funny
Looks for a pike perched on a gunny
To pitch notes to the nightjar
That hung down from a strung jar.

Prayerful trance and a long fast
Sets up a goodtime for repast
For hooded virgins of the church
Committed to save a known wretch.

For the body of Christ washed in sap
Can withstand the cracking whip
When angels descend to bind consent
From congregants waiting for descent.
The body weakens and succumbs to toil
The trail prepares tired bodies for recoil
The otter totters over fodder with glee
To cease easeful time for the newly free.

To Youth

Time is; time was;
But time was enough
To do the things we needed to do
And touch the souls we needed to touch.

Oh, youth! When life is in bloom
Like the open flower and
The dew is soft and fresh
Under the globed sun;
And the festooning stars
Twinkle with mirthful glow.

A time to peel the pitted fruit
Shared and eaten
Or eaten unpeeled;
A time to watch the gyre fall ajar
And the full–formed butterfly
Flutter its regaled wings
To tell all who dare to look,
A new day has dawned
A new era has begun.

The door opens hope
To unchain entrants'
Unchained chances and naked fear;
Lucidness and murkiness.
The murkiness marring decisions,
The decisions that are soon reversed,
Made and unmade.

The outbound thought looks sane
Only to find insanity at the lee;
The crafted cantata
Primed for revisions,
Like the figured fern
Floated on a Grecian urn.

The union of social wills,
The personal spurn of dispersions;
The desire to join and diverge
Fold the past and present into

A new beginning.
The endless struggle of molding clay
Into a flawless whole.

The uneasy parent looking on
The growing infant with awe;
The grown and the growing
Making progress in micro bits
As time on its fleeting axis
Quietly whizzes through the seasons
And leaves us alone and lonely
With no time to grieve
At the cornice of birth and growth;
The passages guiding time
Through easeful moments
And markings that were not fêted.

The seamless flow of eternal time;
The aegis aging the ageless like
An irretrievable note
Repeats andante in monotone,
And the well-groomed goon
Asks us to pause and ponder
What came of those
Who waited on the futureless present
To narrate the annals of change?

The Raven and the Hare

Several things changed and ended up the same.

Trailing and tailing across the open space
The riled raven cannot hear the hasty hare;
Avatars wail to no avail, and
True voices of descent are drowned.
The sign of intemperance hover atop
The white knotted clouds;
The Rufous-nosed rat quickly
Slinks under the nose of a wily cat
And the calm wind ceases to be.

Turning and crimping the unchained melodies
The drizzling rain cannot awaken mermaids
Fissures suddenly appear in hard rocks
The sprayed sparrow spirals down the gyre
To awaken the droopy daylight owl and
The felled trees become death-traps
For the recklessly trusting cockatoo
The tsetse-fly drains life from avid eyes; and
The black vulture blissfully circles over dross.

Erected stakes like frozen posts
Forsook what they stood for when
Contemporary poets cease to pen
About despair, tolerance, and compassion,
Or read letters of cold-hearted killers that
Open a trapdoor for the Labrador to escape
Time without form; season without meaning
The silent ones suddenly begin to bray
Oh Great One, distill our souls
For we are much too daft to feel another's pain.

Our beginnings do not foretell our ends
Neither do our ends tell how we advanced
For both are captives of transient time
The rarely seen and the rarely heard
Alluding capture; the ill-fated muse

Lost to the fog of desperation;
The honed evil slays temporary peace.
Oh! Great One keep us sane and soothe our souls
For our bodies are frail and our senses numbed.

We stand dovetailed like building bricks
Win together or lose together
The strong helping the weak over the hump
The weak looking for hidden measures;
Steeled to resolve; deeded to redeem
The orphaned children seeking pardon
From heartless adults doling grace in tithes
Oh! Great One, keep us safe from our iniquities
For our souls are too tired to partake in the fray.

Neither this hour nor the next is deemed to last
For the moving hand urges us toward the infinite
Capture its motion before slipping into nothingness.
We who are near the shore salute you; we who are afar
Despise you; for neither the agent nor servant know
The passionate embraces between servant and master
When all they know is dispassionate glances
Meant to invoke stifling form over indulgence
Oh! Great One, keep us humble in our delights
For our senses are readied for humor and fun.

The forest is filled with creepy, happy fauna
The wind twirling around roosted twigs
To escape solace canopies provide.
We who are about to slumber disown you;
We who are about to tread open spaces revile you
For neither the king nor the hireling is free
To string the threads of human tapestry
The sinner and the saint; the scum and the scion
The hunter stalking prey; the hunted seeking safety
Oh! Great One, keep us safe from ageless greed
For our needs are few and our wants bottomless.

The Rock

And there was time
Spent to the edge of
The serrated rock.

The rigid, immobile rock
Harbors faith.
The hurried, meandering pebble
Careens on the sodden floor.

The rock anchors the weeds,
The ashy lava, the moss the clay
Of floating household ware,
The broken tree limbs, trunks
The severed, floating leaf.

The rock harbors
The living and the living-dead;
The child clambering its way;
The man dropping killick
At the recesses of his soul.

The rock seen in varied forms,
The igneous, sedimentary or metamorphic;
The friable and graded quartz,
The fiery, frozen and free,
Holding secrets of the wind, and rain
Strewing passages with grainy sand.

A walk to the heated and cooled rock
At sunset after our laboring hours;
The childhood spent, and
The bones weary and worn,

To talk with the phantoms of our mind;
The absence of formless shadows,
The hated hooded owl
Seek salvation from evil
Man can neither devise nor endure.

The whizzing, buzzing rock;
The rise and fall of its echo
Breaching silence of the wind;
Combing the lucid, restful forest
Dousing silence of the still air.

The rock resting on a finger
To profess love that was, is, or
Could have been;
The vows made and kept,
The vows not made or broken.

The Verdin church bells
Tolled from the rock dome
To remind us of yesteryear.
The family and friends that were;
The flow of men though time's expanse,
Resting the aged and the aging.

Time in infinite form
Tells tales of the hissing rock;
When haunted eyes are glued
On the travels of endless shadows,
And all is lost or gained in a twinkling.

The Smile

The measure of the inner beauty is often
Revealed through a smile.

In a room filled with strangers, my eyes began to wonder
Until they settled on a friendly face, so I stopped to ponder
Whether to shake hands with the face as pleasantly servile
Or walk away until I saw a familiar face with a gentle smile.

As I neared the face, I saw shadows fade from the court
Like a clump of floating clouds ferried by a sea escort
Swiveling cranes began to flap their wings at port Kyle
While radiant Venus and many minions amiably smile.

The air crossed the open spaces, and seas to reach borders
Of snuffed men intently holding on to extended blabbers;
Pain etherized victims of a senseless war stacked in a pile
While trowel smothers the untimely passing with wry smile.

A grieved spinster asked the dancers to a wedding feast
To rip nuptial vows written in haste for a groomed priest
To repeat, and return to their humble abodes in a single file
As she turned the wedding rings round with a gloomy smile.

A flower girl who was rushing home after losing a match
Was stopped at the gate to her home by a very angry grouch
And told not to run down hill alone for more than one mile
When it was easier to walk with a friend who wears a smile

A mysterious face filled with pleasant and unexpected beauty
Appeared at the gate and asked about the organized bounty
That was set up for the head of the crook who escaped in style
With Church offertory stored in a Grecian urn with soft smile

It soon departed when an angry mob took over the streets
And vowed to catch the crook with well-disguised treats
But a peacemaker came upon the scene after a long court trail
And asked the group to run home with a friendly smile.

Gloom descended on the gathering at the opposite end
When pain throbbed poisoned darts round the willow bend.
And asked Jim Cray why he was filled with so much bile
When he can do much better with a wink and a happy smile.

Jim responded time had come people to clear upheavals
With a smile and friendly gestures to win over rivals;
Yet wardens from different sides of prison camps seethe vile
When dealing with inmates deemed too violent to merit smile.

So, strangers from unlikely places meet in open spaces
To decide major issues without input from the races
They turned after much debate over what to do with a tile
And stopped when a sparrow soared on the wings of smile

And freed you to sing the happy song buried in your heart,
A pep or so and a caper of two or more that is not too apart;
To clutch the elixir smile when all appear lost through trails
And a deserted child once filled with hope loses all smiles.

The Travelling Seashell

Arriving safely at a destination is much better
Than preparations to embark on a journey.

You look askance when the ocean roars
To end in surfs at the sandy shore
Where tired sailors hold huge uproars
To prune seaweeds for signs in gore.

Did you journey to the southernmost cape
Where soldiers sacrificed their lives,
Or was it to Normandy and bloody scrape
Where honor dangled on broken hives

You sat at the acme of the castle's arch
To watch your kin enter a different race
And gave up mourning mermaids on the larch
Irascibly seeking means to breach entrance.

You used the stern of your plane to jib ships
Whose sails twisting in the summer breeze
Like a spear thrown from the northern Alps
Across flat plains filled with melting freeze.

Dusk awakens you to the twirling sea waves;
The sea bathing debris ferried from hinterlands;
The children jumping from opened caves
To watch seagulls juggling or waving wands.

The sun rayed at morn to remove the blanket
That kept you warm in your sandy bed by the sea.
Or was it the zombie ants using you for trinket
And retuning you to erected cacti close to lea.

Noontide shapes the strings of the turning winds
For the bow of the waves to play rhythmic tunes,
And shape sundry silver plates in scattered binds
That served both northern and southern ice dunes.

You watched the rustic sun bid a sad farewell
To the moon, as it paints the wavelets in gold.
Lovers murmur sweet melodies near the well
And smiths hammer heated tongues in their hold.

You carry your world in your lined hull,
To buffer the ceaseless wavelets of the sea
The hazy salt dust endlessly bashing in full
Erected rocks to hold those eager for glee.

Were you made to churn twigs into leaves;
Pelt pallets at well-dressed reigning queens
Or distill hazy salt for mischievous thieves
Bent on trading battle spoils for spleens?

No! You were made for enchanted chambers
Where Beauty enwrapped in alabaster oil
Entice painted priests to gather in numbers
And tilt their vows to favor alluvial soil.

You know the traps buried at putrid posts,
The charted wavelets moving charted times
Across the large expanse to uncharted coasts
Till you're home and the church bell chimes.

To The Farmhand

Honor farmers
Their toil, care of soil, and
Concern for peoples and plants everywhere.

Oh! Ye lovers of Hungerville,
Ye, with dust-dried eyes and pallid palms
That heed and seed, and know no grain
I come ahead of your homebound trots
To safe abodes and scrumptious meals;
I come, brine eyed and heavy-hearted
To proclaim the passing of Pick the farmhand,
Our dear friend, servant, and companion,
A man, of uncommon valor and vision,
Who fell victim to vicious virus
At the peak of his prime, and
Left us to fallow and flounder.

I come to remind you of Pick, the unsung hero,
Whose ineffable life
Taught us to heed, and feed and sleep,
After a hard day's work.

You recall his sweet smile, and joyful laughter;
His kindness, and ivory manners,
That inspired us to give the best of ourselves
To the young and old, the rich and poor
And better the lot of the burghers in our midst.

He must not be left un-mourned for ravenous ravens,
Or dumped atop pitched pyre for the Eagle-owl, that
Know neither king nor knave, to poke and peck.
For he was a committed spouse and an advocate
Whose work brought warmth to hungry children
And turned mealtimes into happy times
For families to share the big and small things
That nurture, and help them live fruitful lives.

You cannot help but recall his sage counseling
On approach to problems as you traverse life,
Or his visit to your home where
He listened to you and caringly assured you,

Of better futures as you felt a deep hurt
In your gut and lost faith in hope, and
Wondered whether his words were hollow.
Nor the times you went to his dwelling
To discuss the day's events and what you will,
Over a pot of beans or a keg of corn whisky.

You saw him at the family feast
Where he gave you cassava from savanna
And sat in the shade of the papaya tree
To partake in the mooing and spooning of
Mindless prattlers and tattered tattlers;
Intently watch wasted farmers
Hung their hoes pegged bamboo plank.

Or was it at a chance encounter
Where he professed the virtues
Of hearing, seeing, and speaking no evil
About people living in sane societies and
Affirming the good in all creatures.

Or was it in the smoke-filled dens of
Cafeterias, when he discreetly swayed
Authorities to balance law with service;
And patrons deeds with patron needs.

Indeed, you remember him at the square
Where he embraced the tawdry toddler
The rustic granny adult of Paltry Street,
The unbound man and woman,
With like affection and respect.

And, who among us can forget his narration
About the hinterland and the cooee;
The sunray against the Atlantic sea rock
The futile stone-hinge genus,
The equipoise of pillaged granite
Quietly measuring fleeting time.
Or his saunter at a date-ringed oasis of
The Sahara, where tired camels,
With bleeding soles stopped to refresh
Before returning to the sun-baked trail.

He saw the Niger comb the delta reefs;
The Congo comatose at the end; and
The Nile, grudgingly lose its punch as
It emptied its silt onto the delta plane.
He shared stories of the susurration waves that
Woke up the Dead Sea from slumber; and
The unending search that drives humanity
To excellence, and was pleased.

Who among us can forget him
At the vortex of vision and wisdom;
When shame looked kinder than nobility,
He assessed the gulf between probity and depravity,
The divide between the haves from the have-nots,
And questioned the compassion of a nation
That tucked in her hungry children
And hogged grains to feed the world.

Wail no more war-worn servant
That kept still in face of chaos;
Resolve in the face of scorn;
Joy at the throes of misery
And hope in the face of despair.
Roll on to the shores, beyond the reach
Of human pain, suffering, and illness.
Rest in the arms of your Maker;
The finite within the infinite
Who knows the travails of your soul
And the yearnings of your heart;
The intransient beginnings and transient ends.
Sail to the haven of stillness and sound repose
For your work is done, and your rest duly earned.

And rise up from your encasement
Of eternal peace when the of kettledrums
Of your spiritual abode awaken you
Of join in the jubilee of celestial angles
Triumphantly sing the end of wars
And the dawning of everlasting peace.

To Strange and Familiar Places

The soil nurtures all, saves its rites and rhythms
And painfully remembers all.

So, my dear friend, what brings
You to this strange yet familiar place
This place resting on schist,
This piece of sodden sod
This dirt of killing field,
That plucked peace from war
Only to return it to another war
More wicked than
The one before, or since.

Did you see the hard rock
Clutch the dead dry dust
On the wings of Poesy
As the knell tolled and
The trumpeters trill about
Man's inhumanity to man;
The unsavory salt left for
Listless hands to mold?

Did you gather grapes from the fjord;
Search rills for unguarded pits
The slop of irreverently deep gorges
Of alluvial valleys and bare trees
The sand dunes and deep-delved caves
That kept straw homes near foothills;
The pliable pits in porous places
Friable rock set on friable terrain?

Did you come to scar the scales;
Stake claim to subvert disclaim
Dead language of burp and blunder;
Cultures spell and dispel;
Or dare to fuse love and hate
In a crucible of faith and trust,
A distillation of secluded space that
Melt eclogues with simple piety
To urge intemperate youth to use
Land with ardent care?

For as you know, the land remembers;
It remembers these events and much more
It remembers the drenched hate and
The killings meant to save that went awry;
The howling wind that ripped its soul
And left is poor and porous.
It remembers the mournful cry of
The skinny skink and hollow men
Of the wasteland that tore roots
To share with soulless, dying men.

The land remembers caring hands
That bound and nursed its wounds;
The deviants who scratched, and synched
Its burgeoning plants and beloved fauna;
The wayward hunter that
Plundered it for game and pucker
For burial in its bosom.

It remembers the tumid creeks
And the rails of the running river;
The cistern held for man and beast
And the caps it broke to fill trough,
Marshlands and flooded wasteland,
And the hungry it fed or deserted.

The land remembers the rain and the runoff
The horse-drawn buggies and the ruts
The debris hauled into its hull;
The senseless sepsis poised to vent.
It remembers it all, and a whole lot more.

And when the pain is too deep to bear
It cracks and slashes to soothe its hurt;
Oozes lava and heated ash to clear path;
Holds frozen rain and snowflakes too;
Spumes and splatters through and through
'Till tranquil time returns and peace prevails.

And when it wants to be fancy and free,
It lies down for the wind to comb its flora;
Whip the oceans into swerving waves, and
Bridge the budding boughs with the canopy;
Or simply listens to the encircling silence
The heard and unheard sounds
Fusing strange and familiar places;
The land remembers it all and you too!

Zoë tic

The servant is never a master
And the master is never a servant
For like mercy givers
They tug and pull
Until they come to the middle
Where freedom is not held by one
But shared by all.

Rise up! Rise up from your sleep
Ye sons and daughters of the deep,
And break the chains binding you;
The unseen fears freezing you.

For your journey has just begun
And the day void of much fun
To swap the old western shores
For the starry eastern shores.

The grains of the sandy oasis
Now rills as the gates of Isis
The Condyle of your broken bone
Rests in the vales of a pitted cone.

Rise up and proclaim the new roots
You dug from the depth of the coots
The bird that followed you across
The oceans and shared your dross.

For your old roots are lost forever
And your kin will have to endeavor
Without a bright and burning star
To guide you to the land of Tar.

You were pulled from your birth-lands
And tied to the domes of new lands
With whip marks on your bony backs
And briny fixes for your knapsacks.

Hands of steel and the encircling rail
Hands of toil and the trailing grail
The unbounded fear ferrying the lay;
The silent cry capping the end of day.

Your severed lines are lost forever
The clueless, restless wind will never
Join the lines that are broken and lost
Like the biting cold birthing early frost.

The burlap stitched into a rare mosaic
Like the colored ray refracted over a lake
Soon loses touch with its source
And wonders if it needs a splice.

The hands that build the towers of old
The brave who helped to foil the cold;
The hands that picked prickly cotton
Now grope for grungy grimed mutton.

The use of power to gain domination
The dare of hope to accept absolution
The lives lost to join greed and commence
The lives saved through care and prudence.

These stories sadly strew your way
To urge you to bid adieu to the day,
And comb the din for a clean cowl
As it was errant to say what a foul!

Your stock was not one of wanton sloth
Nor seeped in scummy cesspools fraught
With smoking hobos on mounted mettle
Twiddles their numbed thumbs over fettle.

You stood aside for the unjust landlord
But watched Odeon act like a good guard
When the building quickly tumbled down
And hopped like an avid happy clown.

You combed baked-bricks for burnt hay
And the cloudy night for a moony ray
But begged the sun to paint the sky iris
And an idler to lead the way to old Paris.

For the yoke is your unbridled prize
And your prize is right for your size
Yet, in a corner carved for fancy free
Freedom is granted for a small fee.

The past is past, and the present is here
You make the best when you are here
Or quickly fall flat and hurt your face
If you veer away from the rutted race.

Life of joy, laughter, and easements
Life of war, pain and, sad casements
All our struggles end up as they began
A search to ride the waves of etesian.

Life of hurt, grief and tempered hopes
Life of trust, and wins and mini flops
Filled with guile at unexpected places
Gushing kindness in unmeasured slices.

But when the mind is mired in doubt
We ask what the ticking tock is about.
Sunrise hopes appear rather ruffled
And our worth seems sadly scuttled.

You do not desire to shuffle or ruffle
Or ready to sooth tempers for baffle
But know wise-fools use different lenses
To review Pinocchio's scattered pieces.

So, you make choices based on conscience
For what matters is oft the very essence
Of humility's offering folded as a scroll
For telling by a sager on an easeful stroll.

Plight

The endless road of an ending journey
Leads all to the same direction.

We came to life's ineffable altar
When time was fresh and new
And fortune was beaming
Its pretty smile on the periwinkle

You in swaddled love and hope;
I in pickled bane and fear
And like a pair of lovebirds
We rode the trailing winds on
Wings of greed, and sleaze, and feed,
Till we joined hands with the feigning

And as you well know our places of birth
Do not foretell our ends; nor do
The trends distill tools needed to trap or grip.
The usurper intently reviles the usurped;
The coxswain holds to his job at the jib;
The paddler wrestles with a ripped paddle
The passer and the passed tread
The uncharted lanes to a charted end.

We sailed the oceans to watch Poseidon
Comb her hair with silver foam and
Protogenoi bathe his green plane with
Torrent stream of lava, rain, and death.

The pall's fall on draped coffin served
Neither the end nor the beginning.
The avid search for the movables of life
Without a thought of where to begin
Ends when the cresting wave is seen
As a thing of beauty worthy of pursuit.

For, we do recall the pleasant peasant
Whose path we strewed with petunia;
The idler swinging in homespun hammock
Under the scented marigold tree;
The worker who moaned and frowned
When his efforts failed his designs;
The truly free who strode with time
And snaked tasks with unbridled joy

We do not know what became of the urchin
Who brought us laughter and fun
Or the sage who schooled our thoughts;
The flatterer who deified both God and man
With equal vim, and the yodeler who asked
Those he met from Dim Street to remind
Udderless mothers to nurse gaunt children
And homeless orphans to share lees of love
With a defrocked priest serving at the cove

We do not know what become of the light feet
That fell behind the crusade after a few steps
To watch the wreathed life's tortuous trail;
The lot of an envious man with nothing to live for;
The pain of the gentle soul with an unlit candle.

For tired souls often come in tattered roans
To view battered life on the rolling belt
Before breathing ceases to be, and
The outstretched hand says,
"Welcome home from your plight."

The Idler's Tale

Our daily strife ushers us to
Join hands in Odin hall
With the valor of Valhalla.

Work has never meant much
To the dawdling idler
That feeds, and sleeps, and spites
The pleasure and pain of work,
The hallmark or heave of work,
The meager work for mini-men,
The payments made in misery mites,
The ill will hurting all;
The goodwill lifting none.

For the agent is neither rich nor poor,
The slave is neither server nor saved,
The downer or the downed,
The lifter or the abated,
The seeker or the sought,
The avenger or the avenged.

The master is not the agent,
The agent is not the master,
For the master is here to serve,
Nor is the agent here to lord,
The puffed ego that sees no end,
The lion's pride that sees no start
Shrinks at dawn and
Leaves the land to the lustful poor
Seeking refuge from the hounds.

At last, the dome bell tolls
To lure restless souls to rest,
The wreathing leaf lay on wicker sallies,
Knows neither the beginning nor the end,
For the end rests with the beginning
And beginning recoils to the end;
The ringed circle embracing all

A search for lost love despite the haze
The lost that are found because of daze.

Restful moments of idleness that
Refresh the body, and soul for
The tasks that lie ahead.
The efforts spent searching for meaning
That defies definition or approbation
The brayer within asking to be breached.

Oh, the wands we weave and scepter
We wield. The treachery of ill will
That shields boundless evil.
The urge to despise the good we seek
The desire to embrace
The meaningless proxy when
Drenched in self-doubt or self-pity.
Our dash to escape into idleness
When the world appears bleak
And our cherished desires are ashen
At the hands of authors busily churning
Choices for the mild-mannered indolent
Intent on solving the riddle of why
The human-beast and the beastly human
Live and struggle the way they do.

Of Pricks and Roses

There are neither victors nor victims
Crimes or exonerations
But eternal, endless, struggles
For love, acceptance and forgiveness.

The throes of desire lured lust to love,
The dreaded bane tricked terror.
The ellipsoid vanity at prowess
Demurely bowed in defeat
Knew neither our beginning nor end
The scattered selves bound to avatar

We merged our wills at the shaded tree;
The exhumed shards of a broken pod;
Flesh to flesh, ash to ash, and heard
The haunting adagio of the barn owl;
The black-billed parrot echoing
The burrowing brown bunny at work.

The fettered butterfly fluttered
To join the sanded Sahara and
The weighty South Pole breeze
To seed rain of misery and life.
The innocent laugher roiling at the mill
Urging foremen to port death to mirth.

Lovebirds in regaled love tweaked
The footman ringing the wedding bell
And oh, what a muffled ring he made!
Like the verdant tolls for the faithful
To the pyre readied for a yeoman
The cassock adjusting his sock to say mass.

We peeped at the fledgling
The struggling of its wobbly footing;
The hajji wearing burnoose and kufi
Hauling logs to warm the musulla
Ere men from dark, damp cells

Shiver and rattle as prayers are said.

We learned infants were nurtured to live.
The youth was egged to avert empty risk.
The adult wears care-worn face to rescue
The aged, and infirm from deathly deeds.
Life flinted, sparked, and seared
Formlessly across the irretrievable bridge.

We who flew with phantoms salute you
We who drank with Elysian adore you
We who defied the odds of Nike embrace you
We who cheated Hippocrates disdain you
For we are mindful of our place at the altar
Your crown of roses and prickly spikes
The winding road reaching your door
The pinched face and the piteous look
The molded freedom binding none
The selfish selfdom freeing none.

We learned Aeolus scattered petered petals
Of red, and yellow; pink and purple
Crossed the wastelands and bogs
Hillocks and hilltops, ravine and rivers
With pricks hooked to the stem;
The oakum gluing splinters to a boat
Like sealed foibles fixed to stay afloat.

The Misanthrope

Things happened without thought or expression
Often become a way of being without the desire to change
The readings on an astrolabe.

I am the minted misanthrope
Who swirls and whirls and holds.
I am the closed and opened one
Of several selves and no self
Bending with the willow;
Hoarding, and feeding and sleeping;
Like a mouse in a billow;
Saying, "Just fine," when asked
"How do you do, monsieur?"

I met you aboard the draped bus
Or was it the jam-packed train
On a ride to enchanted Elysium
I seated my rustic form
Close to your well-schooled self
To deny genuine love and care
The will to reach a just end.

I am the grumpy one
Friend or unworthy other
A person of no, but all climes
Dwelling with you by day
Fleeing from you at night
Cooking, cleaning and washing
Feigning need to secure favor.

Bowing low to caw and honor
I tip my hat to greet the heathen;
Sit still to soothe my restless soul
Listening for the unspoken and the echo.

After making the bed, I leave it empty
For the groomed child and watch grow;
Look on tattered forms in tattered rags
Float through closed and open spaces.

Aloof like the lonely hermit,
I perch on the painted bench
To rest my limbs from toil,
Fearful of what awaits at the bend,
Warm my hands by the heated lamp
And watch the soft glow of the rising moon.

And like faithful anchored at the rock
I look on seekers of charity
The forlorn hope groping for pardon
The demurred spirit reaching out
When the miter begins vespers.

Today, a man traded his worth for lees,
Orphans sold their souls for gruel, and
The gifted orator disgraced speech
When light shone on his misdeed.
But the well-dressed miscreant
Coyly cracked the best in men.

Yesterday, Care tickled smith for love
Villainy fought the miner for gold
Hatred rolled over Virtue and Honor
The saint's struggles were doused,
The guileless idiot garroted doubt,
And Greed burnt thoughtful Grace.

Our self-absorption exposes our envy
Borrowed friends affirm our loneliness
The gifts of life confound our dreams
The egis of self-denial depicts our ruse
The puffed ego cannot stop wavelets
Ready to crest at unsettled hours

Sunk lives in closed and open spaces
Mirror close and distant mirages
Silhouettes merge with shadows
To rule the supple waves lapping at
The beached debris meant for the pit.

The sparrows sortie for grass and twigs
Remind me of the huddled masses
Draped in surplice of sameness
Craving for a haven to call home;
The hurried step made to fetch or fodder;
The hobbled body readied to start anew
The unkempt life rotting at the rutted path
Where the Misanthrope fuses love with hate .

Stanley Sackeyfio was born in Ghana and lives in the United States. He holds a graduate degree in Business Administration from the University of Central Oklahoma and memberships in the International Honor Society in Economics and the International Business Communication Association. His hobbies are reading, traveling, and photography.

Gulf Coast Publications
Cover Photograph:
Stanley Sackeyfio.

The author believes in continuing the Ghanaian tradition of teaching through story telling. He is available for discussion.

For more information, contact Stanley Sackeyfio at
Poems from Macoma Beaches @ gmail.com

www.ingramcontent.com/pod-product-compliance
Lightning Source LLC
Chambersburg PA
CBHW071350090426
42738CB00012B/3077